FRIENDSHIP,
LOVE & MARRIAGE

Henry D. Thoreau.

FRIENDSHIP, LOVE & MARRIAGE BY
HENRY D. THOREAU AND A LITTLE
JOURNEY TO HENRY D. THOREAU,
BY ELBERT HUBBARD

Fredonia Books
Amsterdam, The Netherlands

Friendship, Love & Marriage

by
Henry D. Thoreau

ISBN: 1-4101-0006-5

Fredonia Books
Amsterdam, The Netherlands
http://www.fredoniabooks.com

FRIENDSHIP

FRIENDSHIP

WHILE we float here, far from that tributary stream on whose banks our friends and kindred dwell, our thoughts, like the stars, come out of their horizon still; for there circulates a finer blood than Lavoisier has discovered the laws of—the blood, not of kindred merely, but of kindness whose pulse still beats at any distance and forever. After years of vain familiarity, some distant gesture or unconscious behavior, which we remember, speaks to us with more emphasis than the wisest or kindest words. We are sometimes made aware of a kindness long passed, and realize that there have been times when our friends' thoughts of us were of so pure and lofty a character that they passed over us like the winds of heaven unnoticed; when they treated us not as what we were, but as what we aspired to be. There has just reached us, it may be, the nobleness of some such silent behavior, not to be forgotten, not to be remembered, and we shudder to think how it fell on us cold, though in some true but tardy hour we endeavor to wipe off these scores. In my experience, persons, when they are made the subject of conversation, though with a friend, are commonly the most prosaic and trivial of facts. The universe seems bankrupt as soon as we begin to discuss the character of individuals. Our discourse all runs to slander, and our limits grow narrower as we advance. How is it that we are impelled to treat our old friends so ill when we obtain new ones? The housekeeper says, " I never had any new crockery in my life but I began to break the old." I say, let us speak of mushrooms and forest-trees, rather. Yet, we can sometimes afford to remember them in private.

Friendship is evanescent in every man's experience, and remembered like heat-lightning in past Summers. Fair and flitting, like a Summer cloud, there is always some vapor in the air, no matter how long the drought; there are even April showers. Surely from time to time, for its vestiges never depart, it floats through our atmosphere. It takes place, like vegetation, in so many materials, because there is such a law, but always without permanent form, though ancient and familiar as the sun and moon, and as sure to come again. The heart is forever inexperienced. They silently gather, as by magic, these never failing, never quite deceiving visions, like the bright and fleecy clouds in the calmest and clearest days. The Friend is some fair, floating isle of palms eluding the mariner in Pacific seas. Many are the dangers to be encountered, equinoctial gales and coral-reefs, ere he may sail before the constant trades. But who would not sail through mutiny and storm, even over Atlantic waves, to reach the fabulous, retreating shores of some continent man? Columbus has sailed Westward of these isles, by the mariner's compass, but neither he nor his successors have found them. We are no nearer than Plato was. The earnest seeker and hopeful discoverer of this New World always haunts the outskirts of his time, and walks through the densest crowd uninterrupted, and, as it were, in a straight line.

Who does not walk on the plain as amid the columns of Tadmor of the desert? There is on the earth no institution which Friendship has established; it is not taught by any religion; no scripture contains its maxims. It has no temple, nor even a solitary column. There goes a rumor that the earth is inhabited, but the shipwrecked mariner has not seen a footprint on the shore. The hunter has found only fragments of pottery and the monuments of inhabitants.

However, our fates at least are social. Our courses do not diverge; but as the web of destiny is woven it is fulled, and we are cast more and more into the center. Men naturally, though feebly, seek this alliance, and their actions faintly foretell it. We are inclined to lay the chief stress on likeness and not on difference, and in foreign bodies we admit that there are many degrees of warmth below blood-heat, but none of cold above it.

One or two persons come to my house from time to time, there being proposed to them the faint possibility of intercourse. They are as full as they are silent, and wait for my plectrum to stir the strings of their lyre. If they could ever come to the length of a sentence, or hear one, on that ground they are dreaming of! They speak faintly, and do not obtrude themselves. They have heard some news which none, not even they themselves, can impart. It is a wealth they bear about them which can be expended in various ways. What came they out to seek?

No word is oftener on the lips of men than Friendship, and indeed no thought is more familiar to their aspirations. All men are dreaming of it, and its drama, which is always a tragedy, is enacted daily. It is the secret of the universe. You may thread the town, you may wander the country, and none shall ever speak of it, yet thought is everywhere busy about it, and the idea of what is possible in this respect affects our behavior toward all new men and women, and a great many old ones. Nevertheless, I can remember only two or three essays on this subject in all literature. No wonder that the Mythology, and *Arabian Nights*, and Scott's novels and Shakespeare entertain us—we are poets and fablers and novelists and dramatists ourselves. We are continually acting a part in a more interesting drama than any written. We are dreaming that our Friends are our *Friends*, and that we are our Friends' *Friends*. Our actual Friends are but distant relations of those to whom we are pledged. We never exchange more than three words with a Friend in our lives on that level to which our thoughts and feelings almost habitually rise. One goes forth prepared to say, " Sweet Friends! " and the salutation is, " Damn your eyes! " But, never mind; faint heart never won true Friend. O my Friend, may it come to pass, once, that when you are my Friend I may be yours.

Of what use the friendliest disposition even, if there are no hours given to Friendship, if it is forever postponed to unimportant duties and relations? Friendship is first, Friendship last. But it is equally impossible to forget our Friends, and to make them answer to our ideal. When they say farewell, then indeed we begin to keep them company. How often we find ourselves turning our backs on our actual Friends, that we may go and meet their ideal cousins. I would that I were worthy to be any man's Friend.

What is commonly honored with the name of Friendship is no very profound or powerful instinct. Men do not, after all, *love* their Friends greatly. I do not often see the farmers made seers and wise to the verge of insanity by their Friendship for one another. They are not often transfigured and translated by love in each other's presence. I do not observe them purified, refined and elevated by the love of a man. If one abates a little the price of his wood, or gives a neighbor his vote at town-meeting, or a barrel of apples, or lends him his wagon frequently, it is esteemed a rare instance of Friendship. Nor do the farmers' wives lead lives consecrated to Friendship. I do not see the pair of farmer friends of either sex prepared to stand against the world. There are only two or three couples in history. To say that a man is your Friend, means commonly no more than this, that he is not your enemy. Most contemplate only what would be the accidental and trifling advantages of Friendship, as that the Friend can assist in time of need, by his substance, or his influence, or his counsel; but he who foresees such advantages in this relation proves himself blind to its real advantage, or indeed wholly inexperienced in the relation itself. Such services are particular and menial, compared with the perpetual and all-embracing service which it is. Even the utmost good-will and harmony and practical kindness are not sufficient for Friendship, for Friends do not live in harmony merely, as some say, but in melody. We do not wish for Friends to clothe and feed our bodies (neighbors are kind enough for that), but to do the like office to our spirits. For this, few are rich enough, however well disposed they may be.

Think of the importance of Friendship in the education of men. It will make a man honest; it will make him a hero; it will make him a saint. It is the state of the just dealing with the just, the magnanimous with the magnanimous, the sincere with the sincere, man with man.

> Why love among the virtues is not known
> Is that love is them all contract in one.

All the abuses which are the object of reform with the philanthropist, the statesman and the housekeeper, are unconsciously amended in the intercourse of Friends. A Friend is one who incessantly pays us the compliment of expecting from us all the virtues, and who can appreciate them in us. It takes two to speak the truth—one to speak, and another to hear. How can one treat with magnanimity mere wood and stone? If we dealt only with the false and dishonest, we should at last forget how to speak truth. In our daily intercourse with men, our nobler faculties are dormant and suffered to rust. None will pay us the compliment to expect nobleness from us. We ask our neighbor to suffer himself to be dealt with truly, sincerely, nobly; but he answers, "No," by his deafness. He does not even hear this prayer. He says practically, " I will be content if you treat me as no better than I should be, as deceitful, mean, dishonest and selfish." For the most part, we are contented so to deal and to be dealt with, and we do not think that for the mass of men there is any truer and nobler relation possible. A man may have *good* neighbors, so called, and acquaintances, and even companions, wife, parents, brothers, sisters, children, who meet himself and one another on this ground only. The State does not demand justice of its members, but thinks that it succeeds very well with the least degree of it—hardly more than rogues practise—and so do the family and the neighborhood. Even what is commonly called Friendship is only a little more honor among rogues.

But sometimes we are said to *love* another; that is, to stand in a true relation to him, so that we give the best to, and receive the best from, him. Between whom there is hearty truth there is love; and in proportion to our truthfulness and confidence in one another, our lives are divine and miraculous, and answer to our ideal. There are passages of affection in our intercourse with mortal men and women, such as no prophecy had taught us to expect, which transcend our earthly life, and anticipate Heaven for us. What is this Love that may come right into the middle of a prosaic Goffstown day, equal to any of the gods; that discovers a new world, fair and fresh and eternal, occupying the place of this old one, when to the common eye a dust has settled on the universe; which world can not else be reached, and does not exist? What other words, we may almost ask, are memorable and worthy to be repeated than those which love has inspired? It is wonderful that they were ever uttered. They are few and rare, indeed; but, like a strain of music, they are incessantly repeated and modulated by the memory. All other words crumble off with the stucco which overlies the heart. We should not dare to repeat them now aloud. We are not competent to hear them at all times.

The books for young people say a great deal about the *selection* of Friends; it is because they really have nothing to say about *Friends*. They mean associates and confidants merely. " Know that the contrariety of Foe and Friend proceeds from God." Friendship takes place between those who have an affinity for one another, and is a perfectly natural and inevitable result. No professions nor advances will avail. Even speech, at first, necessarily has nothing to do with it: but it follows after silence, as the buds in the graft do not put forth into leaves till long after the graft has taken. It is a drama in which the parties have no part to act. We are all Mussulmans and fatalists in this respect. Impatient and uncertain lovers think that they must say or do something kind whenever they meet; they must never be cold. But they who are Friends do not do what they *think* they must, but what they *must*. Even their Friendship is in one sense but a sublime phenomenon to them.

The true and not despairing Friend will address his Friend in some such terms as these:

" I never asked thy leave to let me love thee—I

have a right. I love thee not as something private and personal, which is *your own*, but as something universal and worthy of love, *which I have found*. Oh, how I think of you! You are purely good— you are infinitely good. I can trust you forever. I did not think that humanity was so rich. Give me an opportunity to live.

" You are the fact in a fiction—you are the truth more strange and admirable than fiction. Consent only to be what you are. I alone will never stand in your way.

" This is what I would like: to be as intimate with you as our spirits are intimate, respecting you as I respect my ideal. Never to profane one another by word or action, even by a thought. Between us, if necessary, let there be no acquaintance.

" I have discovered you; how can you be concealed from me?"

The Friend asks no return but that his Friend will religiously accept and wear and not disgrace his apotheosis of him. They cherish each other's hopes. They are kind to each other's dreams.

Though the poet says, " 'T is the pre-eminence of Friendship to impute excellence," yet we can never praise our Friend, nor esteem him praiseworthy, nor let him think that he can please us by any *behavior*, or ever *treat* us well enough. That kindness which has so good a reputation elsewhere can least of all consist with this relation, and no such affront can be offered to a Friend, as a conscious good will, a friendliness which is not a necessity of the Friend's nature.

The sexes are naturally most strongly attracted to one another, by constant constitutional differences, and are most commonly and surely the complements of one another. How natural and easy it is for man to secure the attention of woman to what interests himself. Men and women of equal culture, thrown together, are sure to be of a certain value to one another, more than men to men. There exists already a natural disinterestedness and liberality in such society, and I think that any man will more confidently carry his favorite books to read to some circle of intelligent women, than to one of his own sex. The visit of man to man is wont to be an interruption, but the sexes naturally expect one another. Yet Friendship is no respecter of sex; and perhaps it is more rare between the sexes than between two of the same sex.

Friendship is, at any rate, a relation of perfect equality. It can not well spare any outward sign of equal obligation and advantage. The nobleman can never have a Friend among his retainers, nor the king among his subjects. Not that the parties to it are in all respects equal, but they are equal in all that respects or affects their Friendship. The one's love is exactly balanced and represented by the other's. Persons are only the vessels which contain the nectar, and the hydrostatic paradox is the symbol of love's law. It finds its level and rises to its fountainhead in all breasts, and its slenderest column balances the ocean.

> Love equals swift and slow,
> And high and low
> Racer and lame.
> The hunter and his game.

The one sex is not, in this respect, more tender than the other. A hero's love is as delicate as a maiden's. Confucius said, "Never contract Friendship with a man that is not better than thyself." It is the merit and preservation of Friendship, that it takes place on a level higher than the actual characters of the parties would seem to warrant. The rays of light come to us in such a curve that every man whom we meet appears to be taller than he actually is. Such foundation has civility. My Friend is that one whom I can associate with my choicest thought. I always assign to him a nobler employment in my absence than I ever find him engaged in; and I imagine that the hours which he devotes to me were snatched from a higher society. The sorest insult which I ever received from a Friend was, when he behaved with the license which only long and cheap acquaintance allows to one's fault, in my presence, without shame, and still addressed me in friendly accents. Beware, lest thy Friend learn at last to tolerate one frailty of thine, and so an obstacle be raised to the progress of thy love. Friendship is never established as an understood relation. Do you demand that I be less your Friend that you may know it? Yet what right have I to think that another cherishes so rare a sentiment for me? It is a miracle which requires constant proofs. It is an exercise of the purest imagination and the rarest faith. It says by a silent but eloquent behavior: " I will be so related to thee as thou canst imagine; even so thou mayest believe. I will spend truth—all my wealth—on thee," and the Friend responds silently through his nature and life, and treats his Friend with the same divine courtesy. He knows us literally through thick and thin. He never asks for a sign of love, but can distinguish it by the features which it naturally wears. We never need to stand upon ceremony with him with regard to his visits. Wait not till I invite thee, but observe that I am glad to see thee when thou comest. It would be paying too dear for thy visit to ask for it. Where my Friend lives there are riches and every attraction, and no slight obstacle can keep me from him. Let me never have to tell thee what I have not to tell. Let our intercourse be wholly above ourselves, and draw us up to it. The language of Friendship is not words but meanings. It is an intelligence above language. One imagines endless conversations with his Friend, in which the tongue shall be loosed, and thoughts be spoken without hesitancy, or end; but the experience is commonly far otherwise. Acquaintances may come and go, and have a word ready for every occasion; but what puny word shall he utter whose very breath is thought and meaning? Suppose you go to bid farewell to your Friend who is setting out on a journey; what other outward sign do you know of than to shake his hand? Have you any palaver ready for him then; any box of salve to commit to his pocket; any particular message to send by him; any statement which you had forgotten to make—as if you could forget anything? No; it is much that you take his hand and say Farewell; that you could easily omit; so far custom has prevailed. It is even painful, if he is to go, that he should linger so long. If he must go, let him go quickly. Have you any *last* words? Alas, it is only the word of words, which you have so long sought and found not; *you* have not a *first* word yet. There are few even whom I should venture to call earnestly by their most proper names. A name pronounced is the recognition of the individual to whom it belongs. He who can pronounce my name aright, he can call me, and is entitled to my love and service.

The violence of love is as much to be dreaded as that of hate. When it is durable it is serene and equable. Even its famous pains begin only with the ebb of love, for few are indeed lovers, though all would fain be. It is one proof of a man's fitness for Friendship that he is able to do without that which is cheap and passionate. A true Friendship is as wise as it is tender. The parties to it yield implicitly to the guidance of their love, and know no other law nor kindness. It is not extravagant and insane, but what it says is something established henceforth, and will bear to be stereotyped. It is a truer truth, it is better and fairer news, and no time will ever shame it, or prove it false. This is a plant which thrives best in a temperate zone, where Summer and Winter alternate with one another. The Friend is a *necessarious*, and meets his Friend on homely ground; not on carpets and cushions, but on the ground and on rocks they will sit, obeying the natural and primitive laws. They will meet without any outcry, and part without loud sorrow. Their relation implies such qualities as the warrior prizes; for it takes a valor to open the hearts of men as well as the gates of cities.

Friendship is not so kind as is imagined; it has not much human blood in it, but consists with a certain disregard for men and their erections, the Christian duties and humanities, while it purifies the air like electricity. There may be the sternest tragedy in the relation of two more than usually innocent and true to their highest instincts. We may call it an essentially heathenish intercourse, free and irresponsible in its nature, and practising all the virtues gratuitously. It is not the highest sympathy merely, but a pure and lofty society, a fragmentary and godlike intercourse of ancient date, still kept up at intervals, which, remembering itself, does not hesitate to disregard the humbler rights and duties of humanity. It requires immaculate and godlike qualities full grown, and exists at all only by condescension and anticipation of the remotest future. We love nothing which is merely good and not fair, if such a thing is possible. Nature puts some kind of blossom before every fruit, not simply a calyx behind it. When the Friend comes out of his heathenism and superstition, and breaks his idols, being converted by the precepts of a newer testament; when he forgets his mythology, and treats his Friend like a Christian, or as he can afford; then Friendship ceases to be Friendship, and becomes charity; that principle which established the almshouse is now beginning with its charity at home, and establishing an almshouse and pauper relations there.

AS for the number which this society admits, it is at any rate to be begun with one, the noblest and greatest that we know, and whether the world will ever carry it further, whether, as Chaucer affirms, "There be mo sterres in the skie than a pair," remains to be proved;

> And certaine he is well begone,
> Among a thousand that findeth one.

We shall not surrender ourselves heartily to any while we are conscious that another is more deserving of our love. Yet Friendship does not stand for numbers; the Friend does not count his Friends on his fingers; they are not numerable. The more there are included by this bond, if they are indeed included, the rarer and diviner the quality of the love that binds them. I am ready to believe that as private and intimate a relation may exist by which three are embraced, as between two. Indeed, we can not have too many Friends; the virtue which we appreciate we to some extent appropriate, so that thus we are made at last fit for every relation of life. A base Friendship is always of a narrowing and exclusive tendency, but a noble one is never exclusive; its very superfluity and dispersed love is the humanity which sweetens society, and sympathizes with foreign nations; for though its foundations are private, it is in effect a public affair and a public advantage, and the Friend, more than the father of a family, deserves well of the State.

The only danger in Friendship is that it will end. It is a delicate plant though a native. The least unworthiness, even if it be unknown to one's self, vitiates it. Let the Friend know that those faults which he observes in his Friend his own faults attract. There is no rule more invariable than that we are paid for our suspicions by finding what we suspected. By our narrowness and prejudices we say, " I will have so much and such of you, my Friend, no more." Perhaps there are none charitable, none wise, none disinterested, noble, and heroic enough for a true and lasting Friendship. I sometimes hear my Friends complain finely that I do not appreciate their fineness. I shall not tell them whether I do or not. As if they expected a vote of thanks for every fine thing which they uttered or did! Who knows but it was finely appreciated? It may be that your silence was the finest thing of the two. There are some things which a man never speaks of, which are much finer kept silent about. To the highest communications we only lend a silent ear. Our finest relations are not simply kept silent about, but buried under a positive depth of silence, never to be revealed. It may be that we are not even yet acquainted. In human intercourse the tragedy begins, not when there is misunderstanding about words, but when silence is not understood. Then there can never be an explanation. What avails it that another loves you, if he does not understand you? Such love is a curse. What sort of companions are they who are presuming always that their silence is more expressive than yours? How foolish, and inconsiderate, and unjust, to conduct as if you were the only party aggrieved! Has not your Friend always equal ground of complaint? No doubt my Friends sometimes speak to me in vain, but they do not know what things I hear which they are not aware that they have spoken. I know that I have frequently disappointed them by not giving them words when they expected them, or such as they expected. Whenever I see my Friend I speak to him, but the expector, the man with the ears, is not he. They will complain, too, that you are hard. O ye that would have the cocoanut wrong side outwards, when next I weep I will let you know. They ask for words and deeds, when a true relation is word and deed. If they know not of these things, how can they be informed? We often forbear to confess our feelings, not from pride, but for fear that we could not continue to love the one who required us to give such proof of our affection.

I know a woman who possesses a restless and intelligent mind, interested in her own culture, and earnest to enjoy the highest possible advantages, and I meet her with pleasure as a natural person who not a little provokes me, and, I suppose, is stimulated in turn by myself. Yet our acquaintance plainly does not attain to that degree of confidence and sentiment which women, which all, in fact, covet. I am glad to help her, as I am helped by her; I like very well to know her with a sort of stranger's privilege, and hesitate to visit her often, like her other Friends. My nature pauses here, I do not well know why. Perhaps she does not make the highest demands on me, a religious demand. Some, with whose prejudices or peculiar bias I have no sympathy, yet inspire me with confidence, and I trust that they confide in me also as a religious heathen at least—a good Greek. I, too, have principles as well founded as their own. If this person could conceive that, without wilfulness, I associate with her as far as our destinies are coincident, as far as our Good Geniuses permit, and still value such intercourse, it would be a grateful assurance to me. I feel as if I appeared careless, indifferent and without principle to her, not expecting more, and yet not content with less. If she could know that I make an infinite demand on myself, as well as on all others, she would see that this true though incomplete intercourse is infinitely better than a more unreserved but falsely grounded one, without the principle of growth in it. For a companion, I require one who will make an equal demand on me with my own genius. Such a one will always be rightly tolerant. It is suicide and corrupts good manners to welcome any less than this.

I value and trust those who love and praise my aspiration rather than my performance. If you would not stop to look at me, but look whither I am looking and farther, then my education could not dispense with your company.

My love must be as free
  As is the eagle's wing,
Hovering o'er land and sea
  And everything.

I must not dim my eye
  In thy saloon,
I must not leave my sky
  And nightly moon.

Be not the fowler's net
  Which stays my flight,
And craftily is set
  T' allure the sight.

But the favoring gale
  That bears me on,
And still doth fill my sail
  When thou art gone.

I can not leave my sky
  For thy caprice,
True love would soar as high
  As heaven is.

The eagle would not brook
  Her mate thus won,
Who trained his eye to look
  Beneath the sun.

Nothing is so difficult as to help a Friend in matters which do not require the aid of Friendship, but only a cheap and trivial service, if your Friendship wants the basis of a through, practical acquaintance. I stand in the friendliest relation, on social and spiritual grounds, to one who does not perceive what practical skill I have, but when he seeks my assistance in such matters, is wholly ignorant of that one whom he deals with; does not use my skill, which in such matters is much greater than his, but only my hands. I know another, who, on the contrary, is remarkable for his discrimination in this respect; who knows how to make use of the talents of others when he does not possess the same; knows when not to look after or oversee, and stops short at his man. It is a rare pleasure to serve him, which all laborers know. I am not a little pained by the other kind of treatment. It is as if, after the friendliest and most ennobling intercourse, your Friend should use you as a hammer and drive a nail with your head, all in good faith; notwithstanding that you are a tolerable carpenter, as well as his good Friend, and would use a hammer cheerfully in his service. This want of perception is a defect which all the virtues of the heart can not supply.

The Good how can we trust?
Only the Wise are just.
The Good we use,
The Wise we can not choose.
These there are none above;
The Good they know and love,
But are not known again
By those of lesser ken.

They do not charm us with their eyes,
But they transfix with their advice;
No partial sympathy they feel
With private woe or private weal,
But with the universe joy and sigh,
Whose knowledge is their sympathy.

Confucius said: " To contract ties of Friendship
with any one, is to contract Friendship with his
virtue. There ought not to be any other motive in
Friendship." But men wish us to contract Friendship with their vice also. I have a Friend who
wishes me to see that to be right which I
know to be wrong. But if Friendship is to rob
me of my eyes, if it is to darken the day, I will
have none of it.
It should be expansive and inconceivably liberal-
izing in its effects. True Friendship can afford true
knowledge. It does not depend on darkness and
ignorance. A want of discernment can not be an
ingredient in it. If I can see my Friend's virtues
more distinctly than another's, his faults, too,
are made more conspicuous by contrast. We have
not so good a right to hate any as our Friend.

Faults are not the less faults because they are invariably balanced by corresponding virtues, and for a fault there is no excuse, though it may appear greater than it is in many ways. I have never known one who could bear criticism, who could not be flattered, who would not bribe his judge, or who was content that the truth should be loved always better than himself.

If two travelers would go their way harmoniously together, the one must take as true and just a view of things as the other, else their path will not be strewn with roses. Yet you can travel profitably and pleasantly even with a blind man, if he practises common courtesy, and when you converse about the scenery will remember that he is blind but that you can see; and you will not forget that his sense of hearing is probably quickened by his want of sight. Otherwise you will not long keep company.

A blind man and a man in whose eyes there was no defect were walking together, when they came to the edge of a precipice. " Take care! my friend," said the latter; " here is a steep precipice; go no farther this way." " I know better," said the other and stepped off.

It is impossible to say all that we think, even to our truest Friend. We may bid him farewell forever sooner than complain, for our complaint is too well grounded to be uttered. There is not so good an understanding between any two, but the exposure by the one of a serious fault in the other will produce a misunderstanding in proportion to its heinousness. The constitutional differences which always exist, and are obstacles to a perfect Friendship, are to the lips of Friends forever a forbidden theme. They advise by their whole behavior. Nothing can reconcile them but love. They are fatally late when they undertake to explain and treat with one another like foes. Who will take an apology for a Friend? They must apologize like dew and frost, which are off again with the sun, and which all men know in their hearts to be beneficent.

The necessity itself for explanation; what explanation will atone for that? True love does not quarrel for slight reasons, such mistakes as mutual acquaintances can explain away, but, alas! however slight the apparent cause, only for adequate and fatal and everlasting reasons, which can never be set aside. Its quarrel, if there is any, is ever recurring, notwithstanding the beams of affection which invariably come to gild its tears; as the rainbow, however beautiful and unerring a sign, does not promise fair weather forever, but only for a season. I have known two or three persons pretty well, and yet I have never known advice to be of use but in trivial and transient matters. One may know what another does not, but the utmost kindness can not impart what is requisite to make the advice useful. We must accept or refuse one another as we are. I could tame a hyena more easily than my Friend. He is a material which no tool of mine will work. A naked savage will fell an oak with a firebrand and wear a hatchet out of the rock by friction, but I can not hew the smallest chip out of the character of my Friend, either to beautify or to deform it.

The lover learns at last there is no person quite transparent and trustworthy, but every one has a devil in him that is capable of any crime in the long run. Yet, as an Oriental philosopher has said, '' Although Friendship between good men is interrupted, their principles remain unaltered. The stalk of the lotus may be broken, and the fibers remain connected.''

Ignorance and bungling with love are better than wisdom and skill without. There may be courtesy, there may be even temper and wit and talent and sparkling conversation, there may even be good will—and yet the humanest and divinest faculties pine for exercise.

Our life without love is like coke and ashes. Men may be as pure as alabaster and Parian marble, elegant as a Tuscan villa, sublime as Niagara; and yet if there is no milk mingled with the wine at their entertainments, better is the hospitality of Goths and Vandals. My Friend is not of some other race or family of men, but flesh of my flesh, bone of my bone. He is my real brother. I see his nature groping yonder so like mine. We do not live far apart. Have not the Fates associated us in many ways? Is it of no significance that we have so long partaken of the same loaf, drank at the same fountain, breathed the same air, Summer and Winter felt the same heat and cold; that the same fruits have been pleased to refresh us both, and we have never had a thought of different fiber the one with the other?

> Nature doth have her dawn each day,
>   But mine are far between;
> Content, I cry, for sooth to say,
>   Mine brightest are I ween.
>
> For when my sun doth deign to rise,
>   Though it be her noontide,
> Her fairest field in shadow lies,
>   Nor can my light abide.
>
> Sometimes I bask me in her day,
>   Conversing with my mate,
> But if we interchange one ray,
>   Forthwith her heats abate.
>
> Through his discourse I climb and see,
>   As from some Eastern hill,
> A brighter morrow rise to me
>   Than lieth in her skill.
>
> As 't were two Summer days in one,
>   Two Sundays come together,
> Our rays united make one sun
>   With fairest Summer weather.

As surely as the sunset in my latest November shall translate me to the ethereal world, and remind me of the ruddy morning of youth; as surely as the last strain of music which falls on my decaying ear shall make age to be forgotten, or, in short, the manifold influences of nature survive during the term of our natural life, so surely my Friend shall forever be my Friend, and reflect a ray of God to me, and time shall foster and adorn and consecrate our Friendship, no less than the ruins of temples. As I love Nature, as I love singing birds, and gleaming stubble, and flowing rivers, and morning and evening, and Summer and Winter, I love thee, my Friend. But all that can be said of Friendship is like botany to flowers. How can the understanding take account of its friendliness?

Even the death of Friends will inspire us as much as their lives. They will leave consolation to the mourners, as the rich leave money to defray the expenses of their funerals, and their memories will be incrusted over with sublime and pleasing thoughts, as their monuments are overgrown with moss.

This to our cis-Alpine and cis-Atlantic Friends. Also this other word of entreaty and advice to the large and respectable nation of Acquaintances, beyond the mountains; Greeting:

My most serene and irresponsible neighbors, let us see that we have the whole advantage of each other; we will be useful, at least, if not admirable, to one another. I know that the mountains which separate us are high, and are covered with perpetual snow, but despair not. Improve the serene Winter weather to scale them. If need be, soften the rocks with vinegar. For here lie the verdant plains of Italy ready to receive you. Nor shall I be slow on my side to penetrate to your Provence. Strike then boldly at head or heart or any vital part. Depend upon it, the timber is well seasoned and tough, and will bear rough usage; and if it should crack, there is plenty more where it came from. I am no piece of crockery that can not be jostled against my neighbor without danger of being broken by the collision, and must needs ring false and jarringly to the end of my days, when once I am cracked; but rather one of the old-fashioned wooden trenchers, which at one while stands at the head of the table, and at another is a milking-stool, and at another is a seat for children, and finally goes down to its grave not unadorned with honorable scars, and does not die till it is worn out. Nothing can shock a brave man but dulness. Think how many rebuffs every man has experienced in his day; perhaps has fallen into a horse-pond, eaten fresh-water clams, or worn one shirt for a week without washing. Indeed, you can not receive a shock unless you have an electric affinity for that which shocks you. Use me, then, for I am useful in my way, and stand as one of many petitioners from toadstool and henbane up to dahlia and violet, supplicating to be put to my use, if by any means ye may find me serviceable; whether for a medicated drink or bath, as balm and lavender; or for fragrance, as verbena and geranium; or for sight, as cactus; or for thoughts, as pansy. These humbler, at least, if not those higher uses.

Ah, my dear Strangers and Enemies, I would not forget you. I can well afford to welcome you. Let me subscribe myself. Yours ever and truly—your much obliged servant. We have nothing to fear from our foes; God keeps a standing army for that service; but we have no ally against our Friends, those ruthless Vandals.

LOVE

LOVE

WHAT the essential difference between man and woman is that they should be thus attracted to one another, no one has satisfactorily answered. Perhaps we must acknowledge the justness of the distinction which assigns to man the sphere of wisdom, and to woman that of love, though neither belongs exclusively to either. Man is continually saying to woman, "Why will you not be more wise?" Woman is continually saying to man, "Why will you not be more loving?" It is not in their wills to be wise or to be loving; but unless each is both wise and loving there can be neither wisdom nor love.

All transcendent goodness is one, though appreciated in different ways, or by different senses. In beauty we see it, in music we hear it, in fragrance we scent it, in the palatable the pure palate tastes it, and in rare health the whole body feels it. The variety is in the surface or manifestation; but the radical identity we fail to express. The lover sees in the glance of his beloved the same beauty that the sunset paints in the Western skies. It is the same daimon, here lurking under a human eyelid, and there under the closing eyelids of the day. Here, in small compass, is the ancient and natural beauty of evening and morning. What loving astronomer has ever fathomed the ethereal depths of the eye? The maiden conceals a fairer flower and sweeter fruit than any calyx in the field; and, if she goes with averted face, confiding in her purity and high resolves, she will make the heavens retrospective, and all Nature humbly confess its queen.

Under the influence of this sentiment, man is a string of an Æolian harp, which vibrates with the zephyrs of the eternal morning.

There is at first thought something trivial in the commonness of love. So many Indian youths and maidens along these banks have yielded in ages past to the influence of this great civilizer. Nevertheless, this generation is not disgusted nor discouraged, for love is no individual's experience; and though we are imperfect mediums, it does not partake of our imperfection; though we are finite, it is infinite and eternal; and the same divine influence broods over these banks, whatever race may inhabit them, and perchance still would even if the human race did not dwell here.

Perhaps an instinct survives through the intensest actual love, which prevents entire abandonment and devotion, and makes the most ardent lover a little reserved. It is the anticipation of change. For the most ardent lover is not the less practically wise, and seeks a love which will last forever.

Considering how few poetical friendships there are, it is remarkable that so many are married. It would seem as if men yielded too easy an obedience to Nature without consulting their genius. One may be drunk with love without being any nearer to finding his mate. There is more of good nature than good sense at the bottom of most marriages. But the good nature must have the counsel of the good spirit or Intelligence. If commonsense had been consulted, how many marriages would never have taken place; if uncommon or divine sense, how few marriages such as we witness would ever have taken place!

Our love may be ascending or descending. What is its character, if it may be said of it:

> We must respect the souls above,
> But only those below we love?

Love is a severe critic. Hate can pardon more than love. They who aspire to love worthily, subject themselves to an ordeal more rigid than any other. Is your friend such an one that an increase of worth on your part will rarely make her more your friend? Is she retained—is she attracted—by more noble-ness in you, by more of that virtue which is peculiarly yours; or is she indifferent and blind to that? Is she to be flattered and won by your meeting her on any other than the ascending path? Then duty requires that you separate from her.

Love must be as much a light as a flame.

Where there is not discernment, the behavior even of the purest soul may in effect amount to coarseness ❧ ❧

A man of fine perceptions is more truly feminine than a merely sentimental woman. The heart is blind; but love is not blind. None of the gods is so discriminating.

In love and friendship the imagination is as much exercised as the heart; and if either is outraged the other will be estranged. It is commonly the imagination which is wounded first, rather than the heart—it is so much the more sensitive.

Comparatively, we can excuse any offense against the heart, but not against the imagination. The imagination knows—nothing escapes its glance from out its eyrie—and it controls the breast. My heart may still yearn toward the valley, but my imagination will not permit me to jump off the precipice that debars me from it, for it is wounded, wounded, its wings are clipped and it can not fly even descendingly. Our "blundering hearts!" some poet says. The imagination never forgets; it is a re-membering It is not foundationless, but most reasonable, and it alone uses all the knowledge of the intellect.

Love is the profoundest of secrets. Divulged, even to the beloved, it is no longer Love. As if it were merely I that loved you. When love ceases, then it is divulged.

In our intercourse with one we love, we wish to have answered those questions at the end of which we do not raise our voice; against which we put no interrogation-mark—answered with the same unfailing, universal aim toward every point of the ocmpass ☙ ☙

I require that thou knowest everything without being told anything. I parted from my beloved because there was one thing which I had to tell her. She questioned me. She should have known all by sympathy. That I had to tell it her was the difference between us—the misunderstanding.

A lover never hears anything that is told, for that is commonly either false or stale; but he hears things taking place, as the sentinels heard Trenck mining in the ground, and thought it was moles.

The relation may be profaned in many ways. The parties may not regard it with equal sacredness. What if the lover should learn that his beloved dealt in incantations and philters! What if he should hear that she consulted a clairvoyant! The spell would be instantly broken.

If to chaffer and higgle are bad in trade, they are much worse in Love. It demands directness as of an arrow.

There is danger that we lose sight of what our friend is absolutely, while considering what she is to us alone.

The lover wants no partiality. He says, " Be so kind as to be just."

> Can'st thou love with thy mind
>   And reason with thy heart?
> Can'st thou be kind,
>   And from thy darling part?

> Can'st thou range earth, sea and air,
> And so meet me everywhere?
> Through all events I will pursue thee,
> Through all persons I will woo thee.

" I need thy hate as much as thy love. Thou wilt not repel me entirely when thou repellest what is evil in me."

Indeed, indeed, I can not tell,
Though I ponder on it well,
Which were easier to state,
All my love or all my hate.
Surely, surely, thou wilt trust me
When I say thou dost disgust me:
O I hate thee with a hate
That would fain annihilate;
Yet, sometimes, against my will,
My dear Friend, I love thee still,
It were treason to our love,
And a sin to God above,
One iota to abate
Of a pure, impartial hate.

It is not enough that we are truthful; we must cherish and carry out high purposes to be truthful about ✿ ✿

It must be rare, indeed, that we meet with one to whom we are prepared to be quite ideally related, as she to us. We should have no reserve; we should give the whole of ourselves to that society; we should have no duty aside from that. One who could bear to be so wonderfully and beautifully exaggerated every day.

I would take my friend out of her low self and set her higher, infinitely higher, and there know her. But, commonly, men are as much afraid of love as of hate. They have lower engagements. They have near ends to serve. They have not imagination enough to be thus employed about a human being, but must be coopering a barrel, forsooth!

What a difference, whether, in all your walks, you meet only strangers, or in one house is one who knows you, and whom you know! To have a brother or a sister! To have a gold mine on your farm! To find diamonds in the gravel-heaps before your door! How rare these things are! To share the day with you—to people the earth. Whether to have a god or a goddess for companions in your walks, or to walk alone with hinds and villains and carles. Would not a friend enhance the beauty of the landscape as much as a deer or hare? Everything would acknowledge and serve such a relation; the corn in the field, and the cranberries in the meadow. The flowers would bloom, and the birds sing, with a new impulse. There would be more fair days in the year.

The object of love expands and grows before us to eternity, until it includes all that is lovely, and we become all that can love.

MARRIAGE

MARRIAGE

THE subject of sex is a remarkable one, since, though its phenomena concern us much, both directly and indirectly, and, sooner or later, it occupies the thoughts of all, yet all mankind, as it were, agree to be silent about it, at least the sexes commonly one to another. One of the most interesting of all human facts is veiled more completely than any mystery. It is treated with such secrecy and awe as surely do not go to any religion. I believe that it is unusual even for the most intimate friends to communicate the pleasures and anxieties connected with this fact—much as external affair of love, its comings and goings, are bruited. The Shakers do not exaggerate it so much by their manner of speaking of it, as all mankind by their manner of keeping silence about it. Not that men should speak on this or any subject without having anything worthy to say; but it is plain that the education of man has hardly commenced—there is so little genuine intercommunication.

In a pure society, the subject of marriage would not be so often avoided from shame and not from reverence, winked out of sight, and hinted at only, but treated naturally and simply—perhaps simply avoided, like the kindred mysteries. It can not be spoken of for shame, how can it be acted of? But, doubtless, there is far more purity, as well as more impurity, than is apparent.

Men commonly couple with their idea of marriage a slight degree at least of sensuality; but every lover the world over, believes in its inconceivable purity. If it is the result of a pure love, there can be nothing sensual in marriage. Chastity is something positive, not negative. It is the virtue of the married especially. All lusts or base pleasures must give place to loftier delights. They who meet as superior beings can not perform the deeds of inferior ones. The deeds of love are less questionable than any action of an individual can be, for, it being founded on the rarest mutual respect, the parties incessantly stimulate each other to a loftier and purer life, and the act in which they are associated must be pure and noble indeed, for innocence and purity can have no equal. In this relation we deal with one whom we respect more religiously even than we respect our better selves, and we shall necessarily conduct as in the presence of God. What presence can be more awful to the lover than the presence of his beloved?

If you seek the warmth even of affection from a similar motive to that from which cats and dogs and slothful persons hug the fire, because your temperature is low through sloth, you are on the downward road, and it is but to plunge yet deeper into sloth. Better the cold affection of the sun, reflected from fields of ice and snow, or his warmth in some still wintry dell. The warmth of celestial love does not relax, but nerves and braces its enjoyer. Warm your body by healthful exercise, not by cowering over a stove. Warm your spirit by performing independently noble deeds, not by ignobly seeking the sympathy of your fellows who are no better than yourself. A man's social and spiritual discipline must answer to his corporeal. He must lean on a friend who has a hard breast, as he would lie on a hard bed. He must drink cold water for his only beverage. So he must not hear sweetened and colored words, but pure and refreshing truths. He must daily bathe in truth cold as spring water, not warmed by the sympathy of friends.

Can love be in aught allied to dissipation? Let us love by refusing, not accepting, one another. Love and lust are far asunder. The one is good, the other bad. When the affectionate sympathize by their higher natures, there is love; but there is danger that they will sympathize by their lower natures, and then there is lust. It is not necessary that this be deliberate, hardly even conscious; but, in the close contact of affection, there is danger that we may stain and pollute one another, for we can not embrace but with an entire embrace.

We must love our friend so much that she shall be associated with our purest and holiest thoughts alone. When there is impurity, we have " descended to meet," though we knew it not.

The luxury of affection—there's the danger.

There must be some nerve and heroism in our love, as of a Winter morning. In the religion of all nations a purity is hinted at, which, I fear, men never attain to. We may love and not elevate one another. The love that takes us as it finds us degrades us. What watch we must keep over the fairest and purest of our affections, lest there be some taint about them! May we so love as never to have occasion to repent of our love!

There is to be attributed to sensuality the loss to language of how many pregnant symbols? Flowers, which, by their infinite hues and fragrance, celebrate the marriage of the plants, are intended for a symbol of the open and unsuspected beauty of all true marriage, when man's flowering season arrives ♣ ♣

Virginity, too, is a budding flower, and by an impure marriage the virgin is deflowered. Whoever loves flowers, loves virgins and chastity. Love and lust are as far asunder as a flower-garden is from a brothel ♣ ♣

J. Biberg, in the *Amaenitates Botanicae*, edited by Linnaeus, observes (I translate from the Latin):

" The organs of generation, which, in the animal kingdom, are for the most part concealed by Nature, as if they were to be ashamed of, in the vegetable kingdom are exposed to the eyes of all; and, when the nuptials of plants are celebrated, it is wonderful what delight they afford to the beholder, refreshing the senses with the most agreeable color and the sweetest odor; and, at the same time, bees and other insects, not to mention the humming-bird, extract honey from their nectaries, and gather wax from their effete pollen." Linnaeus himself calls the calyx the thalamus, or bridal chamber; and the corolla the aulaeum, or tapestry of it, and proceeds to explain thus every part of the flower.

Who knows but evil spirits might corrupt the flowers themselves, rob them of their fragrance and their fair hues, and turn their marriage into a secret shame and defilement? Already they are of various qualities, and there is one whose nuptials fill the lowlands in June with the odor of carrion. The intercourse of the sexes, I have dreamed, is incredibly beautiful, too fair to be remembered. I have had thoughts about it, but they are among the most fleeting and irrecoverable in my experience. It is strange that men will talk of miracles, revelation, inspiration, and the like, as things past, while love remains.

A true marriage will differ in no wise from illumination. In all perception of the truth there is a divine ecstacy, an inexpressible delirium of joy, as when a youth embraces his betrothed virgin. The ultimate delights of a true marriage are one with this.

No wonder that out of such a union, not as end, but as accompaniment, comes the undying race of men. The womb is a most fertile soil.

Some have asked if the stock of men could not be improved—if they could not be bred as cattle. Let pure Love be purified, and all the rest will follow. A pure Love is thus, indeed, the panacea for all the ills of the world.

The only excuse for reproduction is improvement. Nature abhors repetition. Beasts merely propagate their kind; but the offspring of noble men and women will be superior to themselves, as their aspirations are. By their fruits ye shall know them.

HENRY D. THOREAU

THOREAU

SEEING how all the world's ways came to nought
And how Death's one decree merged all degrees,
    He chose to pass his time with birds and trees,
    Reduced his life to sane necessities:
Plain meat and drink and sleep and noble thought.
    And the plump kine which waded to the knees
    Through the lush grass, knowing the luxuries
    Of succulent mouthfuls, had our gold-disease
As much as he, who only Nature sought.

Who gives up much the gods give more in turn:
    The music of the spheres for dross of gold;
For o'er officious cares flame-songs that burn
    Their pathway through the years and never old.
And he who shunned vain cares and vainer strife
    Found an eternity in one short life.

HENRY D. THOREAU

AS a rule, the man who can do all things equally well is a very mediocre individual. Those who stand out before a groping world as beaconlights were men of great faults and unequal performances. It is quite needless to add that they do not live on account of their faults or imperfections, but in spite of them.

Henry David Thoreau's place in the common heart of humanity grows firmer and more secure as the seasons pass, and his life proves for us again the paradoxical fact that the only men who really succeed are those who fail.

Thoreau's obscurity, his poverty, his lack of public recognition in life, either as a writer or lecturer, his rejection as a lover, his failure in business, and his early death, form a combination of calamities that make him as immortal as a martyr. Especially does an early death sanctify all and make the record complete, but the death of a naturalist, while right at the height of his ability to see and enjoy—death from tuberculosis of a man who lived most of the time in open air—these things array us on the side of the man 'gainst unkind fate, and cement our sympathy and love.

Nature's care forever is for the species, and the individual is sacrificed without ruth, that the race may live and progress. This dumb indifference of Nature to the individual—this apparent contempt for the man—seems to prove that the individual is only a phenomenon. Man is merely a manifestation, a symptom, a symbol, and his quick passing proves that he is n't the Thing. Nature does not care for him—she produces a million beings in order to get one who has thoughts—all are swept into the dust-pan of oblivion but the one who thinks; he alone lives, embalmed in the memories of generations unborn. The Thoreau race is dead. In Sleepy Hollow Cemetery at Concord there is a monument marking a row of mounds where a half-dozen Thoreaus rest. The inscriptions are all of one size, but the name of one Thoreau alone lives, and he lives because he had thoughts and expressed them.

One of the most insistent errors ever put out was that statement of Rousseau, paraphrased in part by T. Jefferson, that all men are born free and equal. No man was ever born free, and none are equal, and would not remain so an hour, even if Jove, through caprice, should make them so.

If any of the tribe of Thoreau gets into Elysium it will be by tagging close to the only man among them who glorified his Maker by using his reason. Nothing should be claimed as truth that can not be demonstrated, but as a hypothesis (borrowed from Henry Thoreau) I give you this: Man is only the tool or vehicle—Mind alone is immortal—thought is the Thing.

HEREDITY does not account for the evolution of Henry Thoreau. His father was of French descent—a plain, stolid, little man, who settled in Concord with his parents when a child; later he tried business in Boston, but the march of commerce resolved itself into a double-quick, and John Thoreau dropped out of line, and turned to the country village of Concord, where he hoped that between making lead-pencils and gardening he might secure a living.

He moved better than he knew.

John Thoreau's wife was Cynthia Dunbar, a tall and handsome woman, with a ready tongue and nimble wit. Her attentions were largely occupied in looking after the affairs of the neighbors, and as the years went by her voice took on the good old metallic twang of the person who discusses people, not principles.

Henry Thoreau was the third child in the family of seven. He was born in an old house on the Virginia Road, Concord, about a mile and a half from the village. This house was the home of Mrs. Thoreau's mother, but the Thoreaus had taken refuge there, temporarily, to escape a financial blizzard which seems to have hit no one else but themselves.

John Thoreau was assisted in the pencil-making by the whole family. The Thoreaus used to sell their pencils down at Cambridge, fifteen miles away, and Harvard professors, for the most part, used the Concord article in jotting down their sublime thoughts. At ten years of age, Thoreau had a furtive eye on Harvard, directed thither, they say, by his mother. All the best people in Concord, who had sons, sent them to Harvard—why should n't the Thoreaus? The spirit of emulation and family pride were at work.

Henry was educated principally because he was n't very strong, nor was he on good terms with work, and these are classic reasons for imparting classical education to youth, aspiring or otherwise.

The Concord Academy prepared Henry for college, and when he was sixteen, he trudged off to Cambrige and was duly entered in the Harvard Class of Eighteen Hundred Thirty-seven. At Harvard his cosmos seemed to be of such a slatey-gray that no one said, "Go to—we will observe this youth and write anecdotes about him, for he is going to be a great man." The very few in his class who remembered him wrote their reminiscences long years afterward, with memories refreshed by magazine accounts written by pious pilgrims from Michigan.

In college pranks and popular amusements he took no part, neither was he a "grind," for he impressed himself on no teacher or professor so that they opened their mouths and made prophecies.

Once safely through college, and standing on the threshold (I trust I use the right expression), Henry Thoreau refused to accept his diploma and pay five dollars for it—he said it was n't worth the money ♣ ♣

In his *Walden*, Thoreau expresses his opinion of college training this way: "If I wished a boy to know something about the arts and sciences I would not pursue the common course, which is merely to send him into the neighborhood of some professor, where everything is professed and practised but the art of life. To my astonishment, I was informed when I left college that I had studied navigation! Why, if I had taken one turn down the harbor I would have known more about it."

It is well to remember, however, that Thoreau had no ambitions to become a navigator. His mission was simply to paddle his own canoe on Walden Pond and Concord River. The men who really launched him on his voyage of discovery were Ellery Channing and Ralph Waldo Emerson—both Harvard men. Had he not been a college man, it is quite probable he would never have caught the speaker's eye. His efforts in working his way through college, assisted by his poverty-stricken parents, proved his quality. And as for his life in a shanty on the shores of Walden Pond, the occurrence is too commonplace to mention, were it not for the fact that the solitary occupant of the shanty was a Harvard graduate who used no tobacco 🐌 🐌

Harvard prepares a youth for life—but here is a man who, having prepared for life, deliberately turns his back on life and lives in the woods.

A genuine woodsman is no curiosity, but a civilized woodsman is. The tendency of colleges is to turn men from Nature to books; from bonfires to stoves, steam-heat and cash-registers; but Thoreau, by reversing all rules, suddenly found himself, and others, explaining his position in print.

Harvard supplied him the alternating current; he influenced the people in his environment, and he was influenced by his environment.

But without Harvard there would have been no Thoreau. Having earned his diploma, he had the privilege of declining it; and having gone to college, it was his right to affirm the emptiness of the classics. Only the man with a goodly bank-balance can wear rags with impunity.

JOHN THOREAU made his lead-pencils and peddled them out, and we hear of his saying, "Pencils, I fear, are going out of fashion—people are buying nothing but these miserable new-fangled steel pens." When called upon to surrender, Paul Jones replied, "We have n't yet begun to fight." The truth was, the people had not really begun to use pencils. Pencils were n't going out of fashion, but John Thoreau was. The poor man moved here and there, evicted by rapacious landlords and taken in by his relatives, who did n't care whether he was a stranger or not. If he owed them ten dollars, they took fifty dollars' worth of pencils and called it square.

Then they undersold John one-half, and he said times were scarce.

This, it need not be explained, was in Massachusetts 🐦 🐦

A hundred years ago these men who whittled useful things out of wood during the long Winter days were everywhere in New England. The sons of these men invented machines to make the same things, and thus were started the New England manufactories. It was brains against hands, cleverness against skill, initiative against plodding industry. And the man who can tell of the sorrow and suffering of all those industrious sparrows that were caught and wound around flying shuttles, or stamped beneath the swift presses of invention, has n't yet been born. God does n't seem to care for sparrows—three-fourths of all that are hatched die in the nest or fall fluttering to the ground and perish, Grant Allen says.

Comparatively few persons can adjust themselves happily to new conditions—the rest are pushed and broken and bent—and die.

When Dixon and Faber invented machines that could be fed automatically, and turn out more pencils in a day than John Thoreau could in a year, John was out of the game.

John had brought up his children to work, and Henry became an expert pencil-maker. Henry, we say, should have found employment with Faber & Co., as foreman, or else evaded their patents and made a pencil-machine of his own. Instead, however, he settled down and made pencils just like his father used to make, and in the same way. He peddled out a few to his friends, but his business instinct was shown in that he himself tells how one year he made a thousand dollars' worth of pencils, but was obliged to sacrifice them all to cancel a debt of one hundred dollars.

And yet there are people who declare that genius is not transmissible.

John Thoreau failed at pencil-making, but Henry Thoreau failed because he played the flute morning, noon and night, and went singing the immunity of Pan. He fished, and tramped the woods and fields, looking, listening, dreaming and thinking.

At Keswick, where the water comes down at Ladore, there is a pencil-factory that has been there since the days of William the Conqueror. The wife of Coleridge used to work there and get money that supported her philosopher-husband and their children. Southey lived near, and became Poet Laureate of England through the right exercise of

Keswick pencils; Wordsworth lived only a few miles away, and once he brought over Charles and Mary Lamb, and bought pencils for both, with their names stamped on them. The good old man who now keeps the pencil-factory explained these things to me, and also explained the direct relationship of good lead-pencils to literature, but I do not remember what it was.

If Henry Thoreau had held on a few years, until the pilgrims began to arrive at Concord, he could have gotten rich selling souvenir pencils. But he just dozed and dreamed and tramped and philosophized; and when he wrote he used an eagle's quill, with ink he himself distilled from elderberries, and, at first, birch bark sufficed for paper. "Wild men and wild things are the only ones that have life in abundance," he used to say.

BROOK FARM was a serious, sober experiment inaugurated by the Reverend George Ripley, with intent to live the ideal life—the life of useful effort, direct honesty, simplicity and high thinking. Thoreau, however, could not be induced to join the community—he thought too much of his liberty to entrust it to a committee. He was interested in the experiment, but not enough to visit the experimenters. Emerson looked in on them, remained one night, and went back home to continue his essay on Idealism.

Hawthorne remained long enough to get material

for his *Blithedale Romance*, Margaret Fuller secured good copy and the cordial and lifelong dislike of Hawthorne, all through misprized love, alas! George William Curtis and Charles Dana graduated out of Brook Farm, and went down to New York to make goodly successes in the great game of life ♠ ♠

At Brook Farm they succeeded in the high thinking all right, but the entrepreneur is quite as necessary as the poet—and a little more so. Brook Farm had no business head, and things unfit fall into natural dissolution. But the enterprise did not fail any more than a rotting log fails, when it nourishes a bank of violets. The results of Brook Farm's high thinking have passed into the world's treasury, smelted largely by Emerson and Thoreau, who were not there ♠ ♠

IMMANUEL KANT has been called the father of the Transcendentalists of modern times: but Socrates and his pupil, Plato, so far as we know, were the first of the race.

Neither buzzing bluebottles nor the fall of dynasties disturbed them. " The soul is everything," said Plato. " The soul knows all things," says Emerson. In every century a few men have lived who knew the value of plain living and high thinking, and very often the men who reversed the maxim have passed them the hemlock.

All those sects known as Primitive Christians represent variations of the idea—Quakers, Mennonites, Communists, Shakers and Dunkards!

A Transcendentalist is a Dukhobortsi with a college education. A Quaker with an artistic bias evolves into a Pre-raphaelite, and lo! we have *News from Nowhere*, *A Dream of John Ball*, Merton Abbey, Kelmscott, and half a world is touched and tinted by the simplicity, sterling honesty and genuineness of one man.

George Ripley, Bronson Alcott, and Ralph Waldo Emerson evolved New England Transcendentalism, and very early Henry Thoreau added a few bars of harmonious discords to the symphony. Horace Greeley once contended, in a *Tribune* editorial, that Sam Staples, the bumbailiff who locked Thoreau behind the bars, was an important factor in the New England renaissance, and as such should be immortalized by a statue made of punk, set up on Boston Common for the delectation of beaneaters. I fear me Horace was a joker.

California quail are quite different from the quail of New York State, and naturalists tell us that this is caused by a difference in environment—quail being a product of the soil and climate.

And man is a product of soil and climate—for only in a certain soil can you produce a certain type of man. As a whole, this world is better adapted for the production of fish than of genius—most of the really good climate falls on the sea. Christian Scientists are really Transcendentalists whose distinguishing point is that they secrete millinery—California quail with tints of rainbow hue and variegated topknots, Balboaic instincts well defined ❧ ❧

LET this fact stand: it was Emerson who made Concord. He saw it first: he was on the ground, and the place was his by right of discovery, the title strengthened by the fact that four of his ancestors had been Concord clergymen, and the most excellent and venerable Doctor Ripley was a near kinsman.

Concord and Emerson, as early as Eighteen Hundred Forty, when Emerson was thirty-seven years old, were synonymous. He had defied the traditions of Harvard, been excommunicated by his Alma Mater, published his pantheistic *Essay on Nature*, and his thin little books and sermons had been placed on the Boston *Index Expurgatorius*.

Through it all he had remained gentle, smiling, sympathetic, unresentful.

The world can never spare the man who does his work and holds his peace. Emerson was being lifted up, and souls were being drawn unto him.

In Eighteen Hundred Forty, Bronson Alcott, the American Socrates, with his interesting family, moved to Concord, drawn thither by the magnet of Emerson's personality. Louisa wore short dresses, and used to pick wild blackberries and sell them to the Emersons and get goodly reward in silver, and kindly smiles, and pats on her brown head by the hand that wrote *Compensation*.

Alcott was a great, honest, sincere soul, and a true anarch, for he took his own wherever he saw it. He used to run his wheelbarrow into Emerson's garden and load it up with potatoes, cabbages or turnips, and once, in response to a hint that the vegetables were private property, the old man somewhat petulantly exclaimed, " I need them!— I need them! "

And that was all: anything that any man needed was his by divine right. And the consistency of Alcott's philosophy was shown in that he never took anything or any more than he needed, and if he had something that you needed you were certainly welcome to it. If Alcott helped himself to the thrifty Emerson's vegetables, both Emerson and Thoreau helped themselves to Alcott's ideas.

Once a wagonload of wood broke down in front of Alcott's house, and the farmer unhitched his horses and went on to the village to procure a new wheel. Before he got back Alcott had carried every stick of the combustibles into his own woodshed. " Providence remembers us! " he said. His faith was sublime 🐾 🐾

When all the world reaches the Alcott stage there will be no need of soldiers, policemen, night-watchmen, or bolts, bars and locks.

In Eighteen Hundred Forty, Nathaniel Hawthorne came to Concord from Salem, where he had resigned his clerkship in the custom-house, that he might devote all his time to literature. He moved into the Old Manse, just vacated by Doctor Ripley, who had gone a' Brook-Farming—the Old Manse where Emerson himself once lived. Elizabeth Peabody, the talented sister of Hawthorne's wife, lived at a convenient distance, and to her Hawthorne read most of his manuscript, for I need not explain that literature is not literature until it is read aloud and reflected back by a sympathetic, discerning mind. Literature is a collaboration between the reader and the listener.

Margaret Fuller, with her tragic life-story still un-wound, lived hard by, and Hawthorne had already worked her up into copy as *Zenobia*. Margaret's sister, Ellen, had married Ellery Channing, the closest, warmest friend that Henry Thoreau ever knew. The gossips arranged a double wedding, with Henry and Margaret as the other principals, but when inter-viewed on the theme, Henry had merely shaken his head and said, '' In the first place, Margaret Fuller is not fool enough to marry me; and second, I am not fool enough to marry her.''

An Irishman who saw Thoreau in the field, making a minute in his notebook, took it for granted that he was casting up his wages, and inquired what they came to. It was a peculiar farmhand who cared more for ideas than for wages.

George William Curtis was also a farmhand out on the Lowell Road, but came into town Saturday

evenings—taking a swim in the river on the way—
to attend the philosophical conferences at Emerson's
house, and then went off and made gentle fun of them.
Little Doctor Holmes occasionally drove out from
Boston to Concord in a one-horse chaise; James
Russell Lowell had walked over from Cambridge;
and Longfellow had invited all hands to a birth-
day fete on his lawn at Cambridge, but Thoreau had
declined, for himself, saying he had to look after
his pond-lilies and the field-mice on Bedford flats.
Thoreau, at this time, was a member of Emerson's
household, and in a letter Emerson says, '' He has
his board for what labor he chooses to do; he is a
great benefactor and physician to me, for he is an
indefatigable and skilful laborer, besides being a
scholar and a poet, and as full of promise as a
young apple-tree.''
And again, in a letter to Carlyle, '' One reader and
friend of yours dwells in my household, Henry
Thoreau, a poet whom you may one day be proud of
—a noble, manly youth, full of melodies and
invention. We work together day by day in my
garden, and I grow well and strong.''
To work and talk is the true way to acquire an
education. All of our best things are done inci-
dentally—not in cold blood. Hawthorne says in his
Journal that most of Emerson's and Thoreau's
farming was done leaning on the hoehandles, while
Alcott sat on the fence and explained the Whyness
of the Wherefore.

But we must remember that in Hawthorne's ink-bottle there was a goodly dash of tincture of iron. In his Journal of September first, Eighteen Hundred Forty-two, he writes: "Mr. Thoreau dined with us yesterday. He is a singular character—a young man with much of wild, original nature still remaining in him; and, so far as he is sophisticated, it is in a way and method of his own. He is as ugly as sin, long-nosed, queer-mouthed, and with uncouth and somewhat rustic ways, though his courteous manner corresponds very well with such an exterior. But his ugliness is of an honest character, and really becomes him much better than beauty." Little did Hawthorne's guests imagine that they were being basted, roasted or fricasseed for the edification of posterity.

Prosperity at this time had just begun to smile on Hawthorne, and among other extravagances in which he indulged was a boat, bought from Thoreau —made by the hands of this expert Yankee whittler. Hawthorne quotes a little transcendental advice given to him by the maker of the boat: "In paddling a canoe, all you have to do is to will that your boat shall go in any particular direction, and she will immediately take the course, as if imbued with the spirit of the steersman." Hawthorne then adds a sober postscript to this effect: "It may be so with you, but it is certainly not so with me."

Admiration for Thoreau gradually grew very

strong with Hawthorne, and he quotes Emerson, who called Thoreau "the young god Pan." And this lends much semblance to the statement that Thoreau served Hawthorne as a model for Donatello, the mysterious wood-sprite in the *Marble Faun* 🍃 🍃

As to the transformation of Thoreau himself, one of his classmates records this:

" Meeting Mr. Emerson one day, I inquired if he saw much of my classmate, Henry D. Thoreau, who was then living in Concord. 'Of Thoreau?' replied Mr. Emerson, his face lighting up with a smile of enthusiasm. 'Oh, yes; we could not do without him. When Carlyle comes to America, I expect to introduce Thoreau to him as the man of Concord,' and I was greatly surprised at these words. They set an estimate on Thoreau which seemed to be extravagant. Not long after I happened to meet Thoreau in Mr. Emerson's study at Concord—the first time we had come together after leaving college. I was quite startled by the transformation that had taken place in him. His short figure and general cast of countenance were, of course, unchanged; but in his manners, in the tones of his voice, in his modes of expression, even in the hesitations and pauses of his speech, he had become the counterpart of Mr. Emerson. Thoreau's college voice bore no resemblance to Mr. Emerson's and was so familiar to my ear that I could have readily identified him by it in the dark. I was so much struck by the change that I took the opportunity, as they sat near together talking, of listening with closed eyes, and I was unable to determine with certainty which was speaking. I do not know to what subtle influences to ascribe it, but after conversing with Mr. Emerson for even a brief time, I always found myself able and inclined to adopt his voice and manner of speaking.''

THOREAU had tried schoolteaching, but he had to give up his position because he would not exercise the birch and ferule. " If the scholars once find out the teacher is not goin' to sting 'em up when they need it, that is an end to the skule," said one of the directors, and he spat violently at a fly, ten feet away. The others agreeing with him, Thoreau was asked to resign.

William Emerson, a brother of Ralph Waldo's, a prosperous New York merchant, had lured Ralph Waldo's hired man away from him and taken him down to Staten Island, New York. Here Thoreau acted as private tutor, and imparted the mysteries of woodcraft to boys who cared more for marbles. Staten Island was about two hundred miles too far from Concord to suit Thoreau.

His loneliness in New York City made Concord and the pine-trees of Walden woods seem paradise enow. There is no heart desolation equal to that which can come to one in a throng.

Margaret Fuller was now in New York City,

working for Greeley on the editorial staff of the *Tribune*. Greeley was so much pleased with Thoreau that he offered to set him to work as reporter, for Greeley had guessed the truth that the best city reporters are country boys. They observe and hear: all is curious and wonderful to them; by and by they will become blase—sophisticated—that is, blind and deaf.

Greeley was a great talker, and he had a way of getting others to talk also. He got Thoreau to talking about communal life and life in the woods, and then Horace worked Henry's words up into copy—for that is the way all good newspaper writers evolve their original ideas.

Thoreau was amazed to pick up a number of the daily *Tribune* and find his conversation of the day before, with Greeley, skilfully transformed into a leader ஃ ஃ

Fourierism had been the theme—the Phalansterie versus Individual Housekeeping. Greeley had prophesied that the phalansterie, with one kitchen for forty families, instead of forty kitchens for forty families, would soon come about. Greeley's prophetic vision did not quite anticipate the modern apartment-house, which, perhaps, is a transitional expedient, moving toward the phalansterie, but he quoted Thoreau by saying, "A woman enslaved by her housekeeping is just as much a chattel as if owned by a man."

This was in Eighteen Hundred Forty-five, and

Thoreau was now twenty-eight years of age. He was homesick for the dim pine-woods with their ceaseless lullaby, the winding and placid river, and the great, massive, sullen, self-sufficient boulders of Concord.

He was resolved to follow the example of Brook Farm, and start a community of his own in opposition. His community would be on the shores of Walden Pond, and the only member of the *genus homo* who would be eligible to membership would be himself; the other members would be the birds and squirrels and bees, and the trees would make up the rest. Brook Farm was a retreat for Transcendentalists—a place to meditate, dream and work—a place where one could exist close to Nature, and live a simple, hardy and healthful life.

Thoreau's retreat would be the same, with the disadvantage of personal contact eliminated.

It was in March, Eighteen Hundred Forty-five, that Thoreau began building his shanty. The spot was in a dense wood, on a hillside that gently sloped down to the clear, cold, deep water of Walden Pond. The land belonged to Emerson, who obligingly gave Thoreau the use of it, rent-free, with no conditions. Alcott helped in the carpenter-work, and discussed betimes of the Wherefore, and when it came to the raising, a couple of neighboring farmers were hailed and pressed into service. The cabin was twelve by fifteen, and cost—furnished—

the sum of twenty-eight dollars, good money, not counting labor, which Thoreau did not calculate as worth anything, since he had had the fun of the thing—something for which men often pay high. The furniture consisted of a table, a chair and a bed, all made by the owner. For bedclothes and dishes the Emerson household was put under contribution. On the door was a latch, but no lock.

And Thoreau looked upon his work and pronounced it good.

Stripped of the fact that a man of culture and education built the shanty and lived in it, the incident is scarcely worth noting. Boys passing through the shanty stage all build shanties, and forage through their mothers' pantries for provender, which they carry off to their robbers' roost. Thoreau was an example of shanty arrested development.

But as the import of every sentence depends upon who wrote it, and the worth of advice hinges upon who gave it, so does the value of every act depend upon who did it. Thus, when a man, who was in degree an inspiration of Emerson, takes to the woods, it is worth our while to follow him afield and see what he does.

Thoreau set to work to clean up two acres of blackberry brambles for a garden-patch. He did not work except when he felt like it. His plan was to go to bed at dusk, with window and door open, and get up at five o'clock in the morning. After a plunge in the lake he would dress and prepare his simple breakfast.

Then he would work in his garden, or if the mood struck him he would sit in the door of his shanty and meditate, or else write. In the arrangement of his home he followed no system or rule, merely allowing the passing inclination to lead.

His provisions were gotten of friends in the village, and were paid for in labor. It was part of Thoreau's philosophy that to accept something for nothing was theft, and that the giving or the acceptance of presents was immoral. For all he received he conscientiously gave an equivalent in labor; and as for ideas, he always considered himself a learner; if he had thoughts they belonged to anybody who could annex them. And that Emerson and Horace Greeley were alike in their capacity to absorb, digest and regurgitate, is everywhere acknowledged. To paraphrase Emerson's famous remark concerning Plato: Say what you will, you will find everything mentioned by Emerson hinted at somewhere in Thoreau. The younger man had as much mind as the elder, but he lacked the capacity for patient effort that works steadily and persistently, and weighs, sifts, decides, classifies and arranges. The voice was the voice of Jacob, but the hand was the hand of Esau. That is to say, Thoreau lacked business instinct. During the Winter at Walden Pond all the work Thoreau had to do was to gather fire wood. There was plenty of time to think and to write, and here the better part of *Walden* and also *A Week on the Concord and Merrimac Rivers* were written.

He had no neighbors, no pets, no domesticated animals: only the squirrels on the roof, a woodchuck under the floor, the scolding bluejays in the pines overhead, the wild ducks on the pond, and the hooting owls that sat on the ridgepole at night ❧ ❧

Thoreau loved solitude more because he prized society—the society of simple men who could talk and tell things. Thoreau was no hermit—at least twice a week he would go to the village and meander along the street, gossiping with all or any. Often he would accept invitations to supper, but on principle refused all invitations to remain over night, no matter what the weather. Indeed, as Hawthorne hints, there is a trace of the theatrical in the man who leaves a warm fireside at nine or ten o'clock at night and trudges off through the darkness, storm and sleet, feeling his way through the blackness of the woods to a cold and cheerless shanty which he, with unconscious humor, calls home. Hawthorne hints that Thoreau was a delightful poseur—he posed so naturally that he deceived even himself. On one particular visit to the village, however, he did not go back home for the night. It seems that he had been called upon by the local taxgatherer for his poll-tax, a matter of a dollar and a quarter. Thoreau argued the question at length, and among other things said, " I will not give money to buy a musket, and hire a man to use this musket to shoot another." And also, " The best government is not that which governs least, but that which governs not at all.''

'' But what shall I do?'' said the patient publican.

'' Resign,'' said the philosopher.

Thoreau seemed to forget that officeholders seldom die and never resign. In the argument the publican was worsted, but he was not without resource. He went back to town and told the other officials what had happened. Their dignity was at stake. Alcott had been guilty of a like defiance some time before, and now it was the belief that he was putting the younger man up to insurrection.

The next time Thoreau came over to the village for his mail he was arrested and lodged in the local bastile &. &.

Emerson, hearing of the trouble, hastened to the jail, and reaching the presence of the prisoner asked sternly, ''Henry, why are you here?''

And the answer was, '' Waldo, why are you not here?'' Emerson had no use for such fine-spun theories of duty, and the matter was too near home for a joke, so he turned away and let the culprit spend the night in limbo. The next morning Thoreau was released, the tax having been paid by some unknown person—Emerson, undoubtedly. This was a tame enough ending to what was rather an interesting affair—the hope of the best citizens being that Thoreau would get a goodly sentence for vagrancy. The townfolk looked upon Thoreau and Alcott with suspicious eyes. They both came in for much well-deserved censure, and Emerson did not go unsmirched, since he was guilty of harboring and encouraging these ne'er-do-wells.

Thoreau's cabin-life continued for two Summers and Winters. He had proved that two hours' manual work each day was sufficient to keep a man—twenty cents a day would suffice.

The last year in the woods he had many callers: Agassiz had been to see him, Emerson had often called, Ellery Channing was a frequent visitor, and picnickers were constant. Lowell had made a few cutting remarks to the effect that, '' as compared with shanty-life, the tub of Diogenes was preferable, as it had a much sounder bottom,'' and Hawthorne had written of '' the beauties of conspicuous solitude.''

Thoreau felt that he was attracting too much attention, and that perhaps Hawthorne was right: a recluse who holds receptions is becoming the thing he pretends to despise. Besides that, there was plenty of precedent for quitting—Brook Farm had gone by the board, and was but a memory.

Thoreau's shanty was turned over to a utilitarian Scotchman with red hair. Later, the immortal shanty was a useful granary. Thoreau went back to the village to live in a garret and to work at odd jobs of boat-building and gardening.

Now only a pile of boulders marks the place where the cabin stood. For some years, each visitor to the spot threw a stone upon the heap, but recently the proposition has been reversed and each visitor takes a stone away, which reveals not a reversal in the sentiment toward the memory of Thoreau, but a change in the quality of the Concord pilgrim.

THOREAU'S early death was the direct result of his reckless lack of common prudence. That which made him live, in a literary way, curtailed his years. The man was improperly and imperfectly nourished, physically. Men who live alone do not cook any more than they have to: men and women, both, cook for emulation. That is to say, we work for each other, and we succeed only as we help each other.

Thoreau was such a pronounced individualist that he cared for no one but himself, and he cared for himself not at all. It is wife, children and home that teach a man prudence, and make him bank against the storm. "At Walden no one bothered me but the State," said Thoreau. If Thoreau had had a family, and treated his household as he treated himself, that scorned thing, the State, would have stepped in and sent him to the workhouse, and his children to the Home for the Friendless.

If he had treated dumb animals as he treated himself the Society for the Prevention of Cruelty to Animals would have interfered. The absence of social ties and of all responsibilities fixed in his peculiar temperament an indifference to hunger, heat, cold, wet, damp and all bodily discomfort that classes the man with the flagellants. He tells of whole days when he ate nothing but berries and drank only cold water; and at other times of how he walked all day in a soaking rain and went to bed at night, supperless, under a pine-tree. Emerson records the fact that on long tramps Thoreau would carry only a chunk of plum-cake for food, because it was rich and contained condensed nutriment.

The question is sometimes asked, "How can one eat his cake and keep it too?" but this does not refer to plum-cake.

A few years of plum-cake, cold mince-pie and continual wet feet will put the petard under even the stoutest constitution.

During his shanty-life Thoreau was imperfectly nourished, and for the victim of malassimilation, tuberculosis hunts and needs no spyglass.

It is absurd for a man to make a god of his digestive apparatus, but it is just as bad to forget that the belly is as much the gift of God as the brain.

In childhood, Thoreau was frail and weak. Outdoor life gradually developed in his slight frame a splendid strength and a power to do and to endure. He could outrun, outrow, outwalk any of his townsmen. In him developed the confidence of the athlete —the confidence of the athlete who dies young. Thoreau was an athlete, and he died as the athlete dieth. Irregular diet and continued exposure did their work—the vital powers became reduced, the man " caught cold," bronchitis followed, the tuberculæ laughed.

DURING Thoreau's life he published but two volumes, and these met with scanty sale. Since his death ten volumes have been issued from his manuscripts and letters, and his fame has steadily increased.

Boston had no recognition for Thoreau as long as he was alive. Among the most popular writers of the time, feted and feasted, invited and exalted, were George S. Hillard, N. P. Willis, Caroline Kirkland, George W. Green, Parke Godwin and Charles F. Briggs. These writers, who had the run of the magazines, would have smiled in derision if told that the name and fame of the uncouth Thoreau would outlive them all. They wrote for the people who bought their books, but Thoreau dedicated his work to time. He wrote what he thought, but they wrote what they thought other people thought. In the publication of *The Dial* Thoreau took a hearty interest, and was a frequent contributor. The organ of the Transcendentalists, however, paid no honorariums—it was both sincere and serious, and died, in due time, of too much dignity. The *Atlantic Monthly* accepted one article by Thoreau, and paid for it, but as James Russell Lowell, the editor, used his blue pencil a trifle, without first consulting the author, he never got an opportunity to do so again.

Horace Greeley had interested himself in Thoreau's writings and got several articles accepted by Graham's and also *Putnam's Magazine*. *The Week* had been published on the author's guaranty that enough copies would be sold the first year to cover the cost. After four years, of the edition of one thousand copies, only three hundred were disposed of, and these were mostly given away. To pay the publisher for the expense incurred, Thoreau buckled down and worked hard at surveying for a year ✿ ✿

The only man he ever knew, of whom he stood a little in awe, was Walt Whitman. In a letter to Blake he says:

"Nineteenth Nov., 1856.—Alcott has been here, and last Sunday I went with him to Greeley's farm, thirty-six miles North of New York. The next day Alcott and I heard Beecher preach; and, what was more, we visited Whitman the next morning, and we were much interested and provoked. He is, apparently, the greatest democrat the world has seen, kings and aristocracy go by the board at once, as they have long deserved to. A remarkably strong though coarse nature, of a sweet disposition, and much prized by his friends. Though peculiar and rough in his exterior, he is essentially a gentleman. I am still somewhat in a quandary about him—feel that he is essentially strange to me, at any rate; but I am surprised by the sight of him. He is very broad, but, as I have said, not fine.

" Seventh Dec., 1856.—That Walt Whitman, of whom I wrote you, is the most interesting fact to me at present. I have just read his second edition (which he gave me), and it has done me more good than any reading for a long time. Perhaps I remember best the poem of *Walt Whitman an American* and the *Sundown* poem. There are two or three pieces in the book which are disagreeable, to say the least, simply sensual. * * * * As for its sensuality— and it may turn out to be less sensual than it appears—I do not so much wish that those parts were not written, as that men amd women were so pure that they could read them without harm.

" On the whole, it sounds to me very brave and American, after whatever deductions. I do not believe that all the sermons, so-called, that have been preached in this land, put together, are equal to it for preaching. We ought greatly to rejoice in him. He occasionally suggests something a little more than human. You can't confound him with the other inhabitants of Brooklyn. How they must shudder when they read him!

" To be sure, I sometimes feel a little imposed on. By his heartiness and broad generalities he puts me into a liberal frame of mind, prepared to see wonders—as it were, sets me upon a hill or in the midst of a plain—stirs me well up, and then— throws in a thousand of brick. Though rude and sometimes ineffectual, it is a great primitive poem, an alarum or trumpet-note ringing through the

American camp. Wonderfully like the Orientals too, considering that when I asked him if he had read them he answered, 'No; tell me about them.'

"Since I have seen him I find that I am not disturbed by any brag or egoism in his book. He may turn out the least of a braggart of all, having a better right to be confident. Walt is a great fellow."

A lady once asked John Burroughs this question: "What would become of this world if everybody in it patterned after Henry Thoreau?" And Ol' John replied, "It would be much improved."

But your Uncle John is a humorist—he knows that Henry Ward Beecher was right when he said, "God never made but one Thoreau—that was enough, but we are grateful for the one."

Thoreau was a poet-naturalist, and the lesson he taught us is that this is the most beautiful world we know anything about, and there are enough curious and wonderful things right under our feet, and over our heads, and all around us, to amuse, divert, interest and instruct us for a lifetime. We need only a little. Use your eyes!

"How do you manage to find so many Indian relics?" a friend asked Thoreau. "Just like this," he replied, and, stooping over, he picked up an arrowhead under the friend's foot. At dinner once at a neighbor's he was asked what dish he preferred, and his answer was, "The nearest." To him, everything was good—he uttered no complaints and made no demands.

When asked by a clergyman why he did not go to church, he said, "It is the rafters—I can't stand them—when I look up I want to gaze straight into the blue sky." Then he turned the tables and asked the interrogator a question, "Did you ever happen, accidentally, to say anything while you were preaching?" Yet preachers of brains were always attracted to him: Harrison Blake, to whom he wrote more letters than to any one else, was a Congregational preacher. And when Horace Greeley took Thoreau to Plymouth Church, Beecher invited him to sit on the platform and quoted him as one who saw God in Autumn's every burning bush ❧ ❧

The wit of the man, his direct speech, and all of his beautiful indifference for the good opinion of those whom others follow after and lie in wait for, was sublime. Meanness, hypocrisy, secrecy and subterfuge had no place in Thoreau's nature.

He wanted nothing—nothing but liberty—he did not even ask for your applause or approval. When walking on country roads laborers would hail him and ask for tobacco—seeing in him only one of their own kind. Farmers would stop and gossip with him about the weather. Children ran to him on the village streets and would cling to his hands and clutch his coat, and ask where the berries grew, or the first Spring flowers were to be found. With children he was particularly patient and kind. With them he would converse as freely as did George

Francis Train with the children in Madison Square. The children recognized in him something very much akin to themselves—he would play upon his flute for them and whittle out toy boats, regardless of the flight of time.

Imbeciles and mental defectives from the almshouse used occasionally to wander over to his cabin in the woods, and he would treat them with gentle consideration, and accompany them back home. His lack of worldly prudence, Blake thought, tokened a courage which under certain conditions would have made him as formidable as John Brown. Blake tells this: Once on a lonely road, two miles from Concord, two loafers stopped a girl who was picking berries, and began to bother her. Thoreau just then happened along, and seeing the young woman's distress, he collared the rogues and marched them in to the village, turning them over to that redoubtable Transcendentalist, Sam Staples, who locked them up. Thoreau's hook nose and features could be transformed in rare instances into a look of command that no man dare question—it was the look of the fatalist—the benign fanatic— the look of Marat—the look of a man who has nothing but his life to lose, and places small store on that. "A little more ambition, and a trifle less sympathy, and the world would have had a Cæsar to deal with," says Blake.

Cowardice is only caution carried to an extreme. Thoreau exercised no prudence in making money, securing fame, preserving his health, holding his friends or making new ones. This Spartan-like quality, that counts not the cost, is essentially heroic 🥾 🥾

But Thoreau was not given to strife; for the most part he was a non-resistant. The chief thing he prized was equanimity, and this you can not secure through struggle and strife. His game was all captured with the spyglass or carried home in his botanists' drum. For worldly wealth and what we call progress, he had small appreciation—this marks his limitations. But his reasons are surely good literature:

' They make a great ado nowadays about hard times; but I think that the community generally, ministers and all, take a wrong view of the matter. This general failure, both private and public, is rather occasion for rejoicing, as reminding us whom we have at the helm—that justice is always done. If our merchants did not most of them fail, and the banks, too, my faith in the old laws of the world would be staggered. The statement that ninety-six in a hundred doing such business surely break down is perhaps the sweetest fact that statistics have revealed—exhilarating as the fragrance of the flowers in the spring. Does it not say somewhere, ' The Lord reigneth, let the earth rejoice?' If thousands are thrown out of employment, it suggests that they were not well employed. Why don't they take the hint? It is not enough to be industrious; so are the ants. What are you industrious about? 🙢 🙢

" The merchants and company have long laughed at Transcendentalism, higher laws, etc., crying, ' None of your moonshine,' as if they were anchored to something not only definite, but sure and permanent. If there were any institution which was presumed to rest on a solid and secure basis, and, more than any other, represented this boasted commonsense, prudence and practical talent, it was the bank; and now these very banks are found to be mere reeds shaken by the wind.

" Scarcely one in the land has kept its promise. Not merely the Brook Farm and Fourierite communities, but now the community generally has failed. But there is the moonshine still, serene, beneficent and unchanged."

Thoreau was no pessimist. He complained neither of men nor of destiny—he felt that he was getting out of life all that was his due. His remarks might be sharp and his words sarcastic, but in them there was no bitterness. He made life for none more difficult—he added to no one's burdens. Sympathy with Nature, pride, buoyancy, self-sufficiency were his prevailing traits. The habit of his mind was hopeful 🙢 🙢

His wit and good nature were his to the last, and, when asked if he had made his peace with God, he replied, " I have never quarreled with Him."

He died, aged forty-four, in the modest home of his

mother. The village school was dismissed that the
scholars might attend the funeral, and three hundred children walked in the procession to Sleepy
Hollow. Emerson made an address at the grave;
Alcott read selections from Thoreau's own writings;
and Louise Alcott read this poem, composed for the
occasion:

We sighing said, "Our Pan is dead;
    His pipe hangs mute beside the river,
    Around it wistful sunbeams quiver,
But Music's airy voice is fled.
Spring mourns as for untimely frost:
    The bluebird chants a requiem;
    The willow-blossom waits for him—
The Genius of the wood is lost."

Then from the flute, untouched by hands
    There came a low, harmonious breath;
"For such as he there is no death;
His life the eternal life commands;
Above man's aims his nature rose.
    The wisdom of a just content
    Made one small spot a continent,
And turned to poetry life's prose.

To him no vain regrets belong,
    Whose soul, that finer instrument,
    Gave to the world no poor lament,
But wood-notes ever sweet and strong.
O lonely friend! he still will be
    A potent presence, though unseen—
    Steadfast, sagacious, and serene;
Seek not for him—he is with thee."